Libations of Life

a girl's
guide
to life
one
cocktail
at a time

Libations of Life

DEE BRUN

illustrated by Laura Gibson

whitecap

Text copyright © 2007 by Dee Brun
Whitecap Books

Edited by Nadine Boyd
Proofread by Taryn Boyd
Designed by Stacey Noyes / LuzForm Design
Illustrations by Laura Gibson

Printed and bound in China.

Library and Archives Canada Cataloguing in Publication
Brun, Dee, 1971-
    Libations of life: a girl's guide to life, one cocktail at a time / Dee Brun.

ISBN-13: 978-1-55285-899-8
ISBN-10: 1-55285-899-5

1. Cocktails. 2. Women—Life skills guides—Humor. I. Title.

TX951.B78 2007   641.8'74   C2007-901703-7

The publisher acknowledges the financial support of the Government of Canada through the Book Publishing Industry Development Program (BPIDP) and the Province of British Columbia through the Book Publishing Tax Credit.

Acknowledgements

This book is for all the beautiful, intelligent, extraordinary women out there. I hope you have the courage to never sit through a bad date again, the confidence to love every inch of yourself the way we all love every inch of a Sara Lee Double Fudge Cake, and the passion to follow your heart, no matter what your head is telling you.

I dedicate this book to my ever-loving family who tolerated and supported me through all my crazy dating dramas, the legendary "girls night out" chronicles, and of course, the relationship meltdowns. To Paul, my friend, who always believed in the "Yum Yum" factor. I also want to thank all of my ex's, some good, some not so good—but all of you made for a hell of a good story.

A very special thanks to my amazing wingman, Angela. You are a true inspiration in my life, and I want to thank you for having my back on so many occasions. I know I can always count on you to talk me down from any ledge—and to have a cocktail ready for me when my feet are once again back on the ground. Cheers . . .

Contents

Welcome

Where do I begin talking about this little book I have put together? I like to think of the cocktails on these pages as my libations of life. First, let's explore what the word "libation" really means. There are three definitions for this fun little word, all of them very *apropos* for the topics explored in this book.

LIBATION

1   An act of pouring a liquid as a sacrifice. Sacrifice being the key word in this sentence. What don't we sacrifice in the pursuit of love, health, and happiness?

2   An act or instance of drinking, often ceremoniously. Life is filled with all kinds of ceremonies, and we tend to celebrate these with a *cheers!*

3   A drink containing alcohol … need I say more?

It took many years, tears, and facing fears to research this little book. Not to mention quite a few very rough mornings. I would like to know what dog I am supposed to have a hair off of.

My inspiration came from exhilarating highs (one too many shots of tequila), unbearable lows (one too many bad dates), and truly great friends (always full of humorous wisdom). Through all the good, the bad, and ugly (believe me there was ugly), I learned to live, love, and believe in myself. During all of this I was able to *cheers* every small, yet significant, victory, celebrate every precious moment, and sometimes just numb the sting of a bad day. I did all of this with the help of good family and friends, revealing conversations, and, of course, the reason for this little book, a COCKTAIL!

(continued next page)

WHEN MIXING UP THESE COCKTAILS FEEL FREE TO:

1   Substitute any of the alcohol I have chosen with your favorite.

2   Ignore any "warning label" I have attached to a cocktail. Go ahead and throw caution to the wind.

It's all about picking your poison, breaking the rules, and living life to the fullest (without selling yourself short or landing yourself in jail, of course). No lady should ever start a story with: "This one time, I had a body cavity search…"

There are two parts to this chapter: liquid courage and liquid condolence. Your use of this chapter will depend on whether you are the dumper or the dumpee (through no fault of your own, of course).

It's not me, it's you

LIQUID COURAGE   If you are the dumper, never prep alone. Invite some gal pals over for moral support (or just a few good cocktails and laughs before the deed goes down).

Always drop the hammer in a public place; you never know how a guy is going to take it. The last thing you want is to have to deal with a male emotional outburst, without the safe haven of a ladies room or a conveniently placed emergency exit.

LIQUID CONDOLENCE   If you are the dumpee, first of all, my apologies. Just tell your friends, and ALL of his friends, how bad he was in bed. Just kidding, kind of.

Never ask him for another chance, or what "you" did wrong. Another word for chance is risk, and another word for risk is hazard. Need I say more? As for what you did wrong, that's never the case. The relationship was simply not a fit and is best just put to rest, much like those acid wash jeans from the 80s that you have hidden in the back of your closet.

"There are only two kinds of men;
the dead and the deadly."

Helen Rowland

letting him down easy
BELLINI

1 ounce gin

1 scoop fruit sherbet (pick your fave)

2 ounces tonic water

1 cup smashed ice

Add all the ingredients to a blender and blend until smooth. Garnish with berries or an extra ounce of gin (always the garnish of choice for me).

This is the perfect cocktail for a smooth, quiet, you-remind-me-of-my-brother type of break-up. Feel free to sip on one of these as you do the deed over the phone.

I need more space
DAIQUIRI

1 ounce rum

½ ounce banana liqueur

½ ounce lime juice

8 fresh strawberries, mashed

   (or 2 ounces store-bought strawberry mix)

1 cup smashed ice

Add all the ingredients to a blender and blend until smooth. Garnish with a skewer of fresh strawberries or a slice of banana.

This drink has the refreshing, clear taste of freedom. I suggest you have a couple of these with your gal pals beforehand, laughing and sharing clingy-guy stories.

no more
SUNSETs

2 teaspoons grenadine
1 cup ice
2 ounces orange juice
2 ounces lemon juice
1 ounce gold tequila

Pour the grenadine into the bottom of a tall cocktail glass and add the ice. Slowly add the orange juice, followed by the lemon juice, then tequila. This will create a nice layered effect. If the layered effect doesn't occur, simply shake it up and drink it anyway. Garnish with a slice of orange.

This cocktail has quite a bite, as did the decision to end this more involved relationship (4–6 month range). I encourage you to be liberal with the tequila as this unpleasant event should be done face to face.

Daphne
~~Lola~~
~~Margot~~
NEXT

he called me by his ex's name
ON THE ROCKS
… with a splash of uncomfortable silence

1 ½ ounces gin (vodka always works too)

pinch salt (make it a good one, this needs to sting a little)

3 ounces grapefruit juice

1 cup ice

Shake all the ingredients together and strain into a tall glass filled with smashed ice. Feel free to use anything belonging to your now EX-boyfriend to smash the ice.

Oh ladies, this drink is a hard one to swallow, but once it passes your lips, it gives you the tingle you're looking for. Much like those little hairs that stood up on the back of your neck when he called you Lisa (and your name is Cindy). So as he's trying to explain, while you're showing him to the door, tell him to save his breath. He'll need it to inflate his next date.

please don't stalk me
CAESAR
… with a slice of restraining order

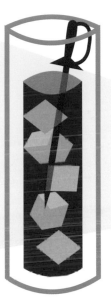

> pinch celery salt (and enough to rim the glass)
> 1 cup ice
> 1 ½ ounces vodka
> 5 ounces Clamato juice
> 1 teaspoon Worcestershire sauce
> 4 dashes Tabasco
> pinch chili powder (if desired)

Rim a frosted glass with celery salt and fill the glass with the ice. Add all the remaining ingredients and season to taste. Garnish with a speared mini dill pickle, and keep the spear.

I encourage you to enjoy responsibly. By this I mean:
1 Change your locks
2 Change your phone number

no break-up sex
ABSOLUTE
… on the rocks

1 ½ ounces Absolute vodka
½ ounce raspberry liqueur
3 ounces lemon juice
1 cup ice

Shake all the ingredients and pour into a tall glass. I recommend you rim the glass and garnish the drink with common sense!

This cocktail has a one drink maximum. Exceeding this maximum may result in ABSOLUTELY having break-up sex. If this occurs, don't panic; simply look him straight in the eye and say to him: "Thank you for reminding me why I am breaking up with you."

I'm going to leave him
MARTINI
… with a slice of dignity

> 1 ½ ounces vodka
> ½ ounce melon liqueur
> 2 ounces mango Juice
> 2 ounces lime juice
> 1 cup smashed ice

Shake all the ingredients together and strain into a martini glass. Garnish with a back bone.

This is an easy drink to make, but a hard one to swallow. So make up a pitcher, put on your little black dress, meet him at your favorite restaurant, and then tell him why he can never have sex with you again. Ooooohhhhhh, that's gonna sting!

my relationship has expired
BLOODY MARY

1 ½ ounces vodka

½ ounce tequila

3 ounces tomato juice

1 ounce lemon juice

1 cup ice

Shake all the ingredients together and pour into a tall glass rimmed with salt. Garnish with salt and pepper and a fresh lemon wedge. The key word here is "fresh."

Unfortunately, relationships and men do not come with a best-before date. So when you start to smell something a little sour, it's time to reevaluate. Weigh your pros and cons about the man and the relationship and see which side comes out on top. Do this with a pitcher of this cocktail in the presence of a girlfriend … now the truth will really come out. Relationships are like poker; ya gotta know when to fold 'em.

"Women might be able to fake orgasms. But men can fake whole relationships."

Sharon Stone

LIQUID CONDOLENCE

so you still want to be friends?
SPRITZER

2 ounces white wine

1 ounce Cointreau

1 cup ice

3 ounces soda water

(use Sprite or 7up if your prefer something sweeter)

Shake the wine and Cointreau with the ice and strain into a large wine glass filled with ice. Top with the soda water. Garnish with a lemon or lime wedge.

Oh, those dreaded seven little words. I recommend you enjoy several of these with good friends at a restaurant you can't afford, wearing a pair of new shoes you can't afford, over an evening of dinner and drinks that will max out your credit card.

pearl harbor
MARTINI
… with a splash of some sort of flotation device

1 ½ ounces gin

½ ounce dry vermouth

1 teaspoon grenadine

freshly squeezed juice from 1 tangerine or mandarin

1 cup ice

Shake all the ingredients together and strain into a martini glass. Garnish with 2 extra-strength pain relievers for the next morning.

This cocktail can be served 2 very different ways:

1   By a sexy bartender (and repeated often). Do so in the company of girl friends, loud music, and hot men …

OR, my personal favorite

2   All over your now EX-boyfriends face

he had his
SHOT

1 ½ ounces butterscotch schnapps
½ ounce Irish cream liqueur
1 cup ice

Shake all the ingredients together and strain into a shot glass rimmed with brown sugar. Do not garnish with one single tear!

This shot has a rich, smooth, sweet flavor—much like the next man who is about to walk into your life. I know that the one who just walked out was not only poor, he was poe, and also lumpy, and sour. Remember, it's his loss! (Much like his hair, hee hee hee.)

plenty of fish in the sea

SLING

… with a splash of hook, line, and sinker

> 1 ½ ounces gin
>
> 3 ounces raspberry/cranberry juice blend
>
> 2 ounces lemonade
>
> 1 cup ice

Shake all the ingredients together and serve in a rocks glass filled with ice. Garnish with a lemon wedge or sinker lure, your choice.

One lost, ten found. You deserve better. He wasn't worth it. Love comes around when you're not looking. I know all these sayings are cheesy and that everyone says them in one form or another. Even though they're clichés, I do believe they're true. So what you need is fresh bait! Go get your hair done, your nails polished, put on a "here come my sillies" outfit, and head out for a night on the town with the girls. Remember, it's always more fun to go fishing with a buddy.

I hope you get caught in a
MUDSLIDE

1 ounce vodka

1 ounce Kahlua

½ ounce dark crème de cacao

½ cup vanilla ice cream

1 cup smashed ice

Add all the ingredients to a blender and blend until smooth. Pour into a cocktail glass and top with chocolate shavings. If the cocktail is too thick, thin it out with a splash of milk, or more alcohol. Your call.

This is a great sipping cocktail to cool down all those vengeful thoughts carving their way through your brain. If these thoughts continue for an extended period of time, I encourage you to share them with a professional (therapist, that is).

I'll call you: Unfortunately, these three little words are uttered all too often as he is picking up his jockeys off your bedroom floor. So why hasn't he called? You waited the acceptable date/time ratio before giving up the milk for free, so why doesn't he want to buy the cow? Has he been in some sort of horrific accident? On life support? Amnesia? Maybe needing one of your kidneys! No such luck. Keep all of your internal organs, whip up a couple of these babies, sit, and reminisce about just how bad he was in bed.

I'll call you

COLADA

... with a slice of *you have no new messages*

1 ounce vanilla schnapps

1 ounce peach schnapps

2 ounces orange juice

1 ounce lime juice

1 cup smashed ice

Add all the ingredients to a blender and blend until smooth. Serve in a frosted, sugar-rimmed glass. Garnish with your choice of fresh fruit.

I'm emotionally unavailable

MANHATTAN

1 ounce rye
½ ounce dry vermouth
½ ounce cherry brandy
1 cup smashed ice

Shake all the ingredients together and strain into a chilled rocks glass (the colder the drink, the better). Garnish with an entire jar of cocktail cherries.

"I'm emotionally unavailable"

TRANSLATION 1   "I still want to sleep with you, but only when I call drunk at 3:00 a.m. And don't think this is exclusive; I'll be sleeping with other people."

TRANSLATION 2   "I am incapable of any emotion."

Ladies: don't fall for this one, it's a trap. Guys tend to think that if they toss the word "emotion" around, we will get all weepy and think they're sooooo in touch with their feelings.

These guys are in touch with something alright, but it's due south of any emotion or feelings!

Please remember, surviving these trials in life only make you stronger. The stronger the cocktail, the easier the trial.

commitaphobe
COSMOPOLITAN

1 ½ ounces vodka

½ ounce of Cointreau

3 ounces cranberry juice

1 ounce lime juice

1 cup smashed ice

Shake all the ingredients together and strain into a martini glass.

Unfortunately, this drink is all too popular. When you have to order this libation, you may have been living with the person that just dumped you. So always serve with a slice of *making him move out,* and a dash of *one night stand with his best friend.* Ooooooohhhh, that's cold.

I hope this gives you some great cocktail ideas and tips to deal with this whole breakup thing. Just remember to always be a lady and to have class and dignity whenever possible. And when it's not possible to have class and dignity, have another cocktail and make a scene he will not soon forget.

In this chapter I bring you libations that have the two most important ingredients of any good date: honesty and a sense of humor. Even if your dress, hair, shoes, and lipstick serve up an exquisite dish, without both of these ingredients, the date is a recipe for disaster.

the dating pool
...and its lack of lifeguards

KEY POINTS For first dates and blind dates, always have a wingman. Bring your cell phone and have a girlfriend give you an out-call. If you're about to stick a salad fork in your eye during the date, answer the phone and act saddened that your Aunt Myrtle just fell down the stairs.

Remember to always keep a positive outlook on dating, unless the guy is disappointing and has not quite evolved yet. In that case, order the lobster and an expensive bottle of wine, don't eat anything, and then blame it on that time of the month. Can't imagine you'll have to worry about a second date.

Finally, have fun. Even if the date is worse than doing your taxes while getting a root canal. At least share the experience with your girlfriends afterwards, (over a chilled libation, of course) and have a good laugh about it. This also helps warn other potential victims about the troll with whom you had the misfortune of spending an evening. Us girls gotta stick together. And since men don't come with warning labels, we need to apply our own: CAUTION: A DATE WITH THIS MAN MAY INDUCE NAUSEA AND EXTREME BOREDOM!

"I drink to make other people interesting."

George Jean Nathan

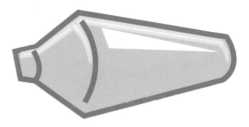

he must have lost my number
ON THE ROCKS

1 ½ ounces white tequila

½ ounce banana liqueur

2 ounces lime juice

1 cup ice

Shake all the ingredients together and strain into a tall glass filled with ice. Garnish with a slice of banana and a ride on the bitter bus.

This cocktail is always served with a slice of denial. He may have lost your number, but he also may have run off and joined the circus. No matter how you mix it, this one is always a little bitter. So add a dash of *his loss* and move on.

so...do you like stuff?
COLADA

1 ½ ounces Malibu rum

½ ounce banana liqueur

1 ripe smashed banana

2 ounces lemon or lime juice

1 ounce water

1 cup smashed ice

Add all the ingredients into a blender and blend until smooth. Pour into a tall glass and garnish with chocolate shavings if you so desire. Who am I kidding? What girl doesn't desire chocolate?

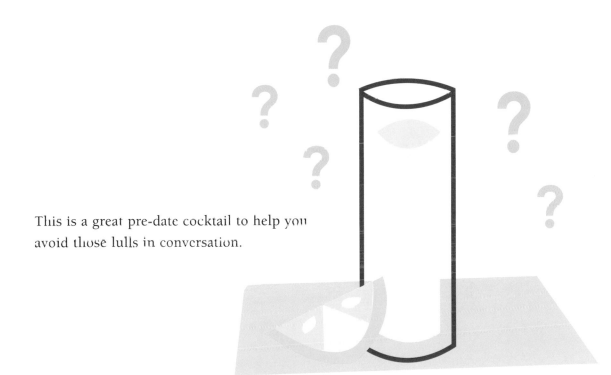

This is a great pre-date cocktail to help you avoid those lulls in conversation.

I encourage you to make up a pitcher of these and invite your girlfriends over while you're getting ready. This is the time to go over what you're going to talk about, brush up on current events, or simply just reminisce and laugh about past dates.

I still live with my parents
STINGER
… with a slice of no chance for a second date

> 1 ½ ounces cognac
> ½ ounce white crème de menthe
> 1 cup ice

Shake all the ingredients together and strain into a rocks glass filled with ice. Garnish with a sprig of mint or chocolate shavings. Everything is better with chocolate.

Immediately order this drink if you hear, "I still live with my parents" uttered at any point in the date. Make it a double, suck it back, and then suddenly develop some sort of rash and leave.

he's between jobs
BELLINI

1 ½ ounces vodka

½ ounce peach schnapps

3 ounces cranberry juice

1 ounce lemon juice

1 cup smashed ice

Add all the ingredients to a blender. Blend until smooth and pour into a large glass. Garnish with your credit card, because with no J-O-B, he's not picking up the T-A-B.

When ordering this drink, follow the same advice as the "I still live with my parents" cocktail. The term "between jobs" can be taken many different ways. In this case, it means, "To mooch, or not to mooch."

he has a great personality

PARALYZER

… with a slice of skepticism

1 ½ ounces vodka

½ ounce coffee flavored liqueur

½ ounce tequila

3 ounces milk

1 cup ice

splash cola

Shake all the ingredients together, except for the cola, and strain into a large glass filled with ice. Pour a splash of cola on top and stir.

(Tequila optional. Warning: creates comatose feelings. Have a good wingman on board.)

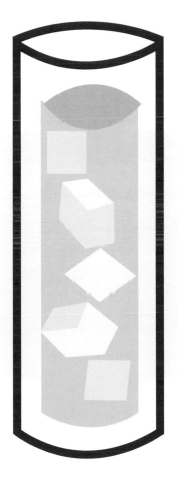

My mama always told me, "the road to hell is paved with good intentions," and I do believe she was right. So ask yourself how much you like your friend that has set you up with Mr. Personality. Try and remember if there was a time you upset this friend. Sure, a great personality is an asset, but what's the trade off? And if your so-called friend is single, ask her why she's not dating him…

delete.

my internet date has a virus
DAIQUIRI
… with a slice of ctrl, alt, delete

1 ounce raspberry vodka

1 ounce pomegranate liqueur

2 ounces lemonade

1 ounce cranberry juice

1 cup smashed ice

Add all the ingredients in a blender. Blend until smooth and pour into a large glass rimmed with sugar. Garnish with fresh fruit.

They need to have warning labels on these sites similar to those on car mirrors: EVERYTHING ON THIS SITE IS THE OPPOSITE OF WHAT IT APPEARS TO BE! Remember, when his profile says he is tall, dark, athletic, handsome, likes nature hikes, and window shopping, this translates to short, pasty, got picked last in gym class. Besides, we all know that handsome is in the eye of the BEER holder.

48

I wanna take it sloe
GIN FIZZ

2 ounces gin

1 ounce lemon juice

1 mint spring (or any breath mint will do)

1 cup ice

2 ounces soda water

   (use Sprite or 7up if you prefer something sweeter)

Shake all the ingredients together, except for the soda water. Strain into a tall glass of smashed ice and top with the soda water.

These five little words have the same effect on a man as kryptonite has on Superman, no matter how NICE he appears to be. Much like the five other dreaded little words men hate to hear: "we can still be friends." Just remember, relationships are a marathon, not a sprint, so pace yourself. You will be glad you did when it's finally time to cross the finish line.

speed dating in the slow lane
SLING

1 ounce lemon gin

1 ounce passion fruit liqueur

2 ounces orange juice

1 ounce pineapple juice

1 cup ice

1 ounce soda water

Shake all the ingredients together, except for the soda water. Strain into a tall glass filled with smashed ice and top with the soda water. Garnish with a road map; you'll need one for this.

Ladies, I can't understand how we magnificent creatures can spend more time deciding on whether to order a fat or non-fat latté than whether to tick the *like, don't like,* or *maybe* box on a speed dating preference card. (The card that was so kindly supplied by the man, who ever so kindly separated you from your hard-earned fifty bucks in exchange for this forty-five minutes of hell.)

I've had more intimate meetings in an elevator. BEWARE ! Uneven road ahead.

he made me go dutch
DAIQUIRI

1 ounce white rum

1 ounce Malibu rum

2 ounces pineapple juice

2 ounces orange juice

1 cup smashed ice

Add all the ingredients to a blender. Blend until smooth and serve in a chilled glass. Garnish with a wedge of pineapple or a slice of orange.

This cocktail can only be ordered if he asked you out to dinner. I am still an old fashioned girl at heart, who believes that the asker pays for the askee. Especially on a first date. Now really, what would your mama say?

enough about you, let's talk about me

MARTINI
... with a wedge of yadda, yadda, yadda

1 ½ ounces white rum
½ ounce Cointreau
3 ounces grapefruit juice
1 cup smashed ice

Shake all the ingredients together and strain into a sugar-rimmed martini glass.

This drink is to be ordered when you can't get a word in edgewise. By this point, you don't care what he does, who he knows, or why he wet the bed at camp. Fake a migraine and take off to meet your girlfriends for some stimulating conversation.

maybe next time
MOJITO
… with a wedge of hope

2 ounces rum

½ ounce white crème de menthe (or fresh mint leaves)

1 teaspoon sugar

2 ounces lime juice

1 cup smashed ice

1 ounce soda water

Shake all the ingredients together, except for the soda water. Strain into a chilled glass of smashed ice and top with the soda water. If you have fresh mint for this drink, substitute it for the crème de menthe. (Soak the mint leaves in the rum an hour ahead of time to infuse it with flavor. Personally, I can never wait that long.)

I have put my lips to this cocktail on one too many occasions. Much like we can't look away from a train wreck, we must sit and dissect a bad date. This cocktail is a great way to refresh the soul and talk yourself out of NEVER DATING AGAIN. After all, the man (and I use the term loosely) with whom you had the misfortune of sitting through a bad dinner, movie, or, God forbid, a monster truck show, is simply depriving some poor village of its idiot.

I'm dating a superhero: Captain Coupon

COLADA
… with a splash of buy one, get one free

1 ounce rum
1 ounce strawberry liqueur
3 ounce Piña Colada mix
    (or pineapple juice)
1 cup smashed ice

Add all the ingredients to a blender and blend until smooth. Serve in a sugar-rimmed glass.

Don't get me wrong, I am all about a good bargain, mainly when it comes to shoes… but when the waiter comes to your table to ask if you would like a cocktail to start, the last words you want your date to utter are: "Ummmm, do you guys, like, take coupons tonight?" I say, up, up, and away with him!

no place like home
MARGARITA
... (and me without my ruby slippers)

2 ounces citrus flavored vodka

3 ounces pomegranate juice

1 squeeze fresh orange

1 squeeze fresh lemon

1 cup smashed ice

Add all the ingredients to a blender and blend until smooth. Serve in a large icing sugar-rimmed glass. Mmmmm, so good!

Order this cocktail when you're trapped in a bad, I-would-rather-be-having-something-waxed, kind of date. Then close your eyes and click your heels three times... still there? Just ask him how many kids he wants and if he's into big weddings. CHECK PLEASE! Works every time.

good on paper
COSMOPOLITAN

1 ½ ounces lemon vodka

½ ounce cherry brandy

1 cup smashed ice

3 ounces tonic water

Shake the vodka and brandy with the ice, then strain into a martini glass. Top with tonic water and garnish with a slice of disappointment.

Serve this drink with a side of ZSA ZSA ZSOO, as there is clearly none on this date. Great guy, good job, good values, no spark. It's like getting socks at Christmas.

"The perfect lover is the one who turns into pizza at 4:00 a.m."

Charles Pierce

he was bad in bed
WALLBANGER
… with a slice of *not tonight honey, I have a headache*

1 ounce vodka

1 ounce Galliano

3 ounces orange juice

1 cup ice

Shake all the ingredients together and strain into a tall glass with ice.

There are no walls a-bangin' here. "You're bad in bed" is truly something you should never say to a man. It has mammoth consequences that could result in years and thousands of dollars in therapy.

I compare it to that question
we often ask men: "Do I look fat
in this?" Imagine your emotional state
if the answer was, "Why, yes you do. It looks
like you could show a movie on your ass, double
feature perhaps." This, however, does not mean
you can't let your girlfriends in on his lackluster
lovemaking. Again, another warning label is needed.

he's a mama's boy
MAI TAI
… with a slice of apron strings

> 1 ½ ounces rum
> ½ ounce cherry brandy
> 2 ounces orange juice
> 1 ounce lime juice
> 1 cup ice

Shake all the ingredients together and strain into a tall glass of smashed ice. Garnish with the knowledge that you can never compete with the woman who gave birth to him.

Remember, there is a difference between a MAMA'S BOY and a boy who loves his mama. Who doesn't want a man who loves his mother? Just steer clear of the one that loves the mothering!

There are no scissors sharp enough to cut these strings. How to tell if he's a mama's boy:

1 His mother calls on your date and he answers.

2 He tells you that she picked out his outfit for the Big Date.

3 He critiques his food by saying, "It's not quite as good as my mother's."

4 He shares a funny story with you beginning with, "This one time, when I was at bingo with Mother … "

he's too good to be true!

TARTINI
… with a splash of reality

> 1 ½ ounces lemon vodka
> ½ ounce sour apple schnapps
> 2 ounces white cranberry juice
> 1 cup smashed ice

Shake all the ingredients together and strain into a martini glass. Garnish with a wedge of apple.

Haven't you always been told that if something is too good to be true, then it probably is? I firmly believe these to be the truest words ever uttered (next to "chocolate is good for you"). If he is that good, then enjoy it. But always be prepared for some kind of skeleton to fall out of the closet. If any man is that good, we all know at one point in his life, he must have been a woman.

My goal in this chapter was to give you a little insight and ammunition to carry onto the battlefield of dating. Just remember a few key maneuvers: always put on two coats of mascara, never reveal too much of the sillies and if you'd rather be home putting your canned goods in alphabetical order, the date is not going well. So don't torture yourself, there's no crime in ending the night early — your time is precious.

Oh, how I hate to have to include a chapter like this. Unfortunately, as long as society plumps, perks, and airbrushes its idea of a perfect woman, we need low-cal options. Keep in mind that "stressed" is really "desserts" spelled backwards. But also keep in mind that a balanced diet does not mean holding a pint of rocky road in each hand. If you're

Trim the back fat

sitting there debating whether or not to go to the gym, I do believe that enjoying one of these cocktails will aid in your decision. After all, they are technically good for you. Why not have two?

KEY POINTS These cocktails are strictly reserved for those nights when, by some grace of God, you fit into your Skinny Jeans. At all costs, we need to avoid a zipper-splitting or button-popping incident.

I'm going to try and say this as quietly as possible to avoid some sort of emotional breakdown that may cause an eating-the-entire-contents-of-your-fridge moment—*bathing suit season*. Shhhhhhh.

These cocktails are also great for any holiday season, to allow a guilt-free hazing of the buffet.

"I've been on a diet for two weeks
and all I've lost is 14 days."

Totie Fields

Here are some fun caloric facts to make your low-cal selections that much easier:

VODKA 1 precious fluid ounce of this clear liquid lover o' mine has 64 cal, 0 grams of fat, and NO carbs!

Now let's compare that to 1 ounce of a plain rice cake: 111 cal, 18 grams of fat, and 23 grams of carbs! Hmmmmm, tough choice. I'll have mine with tonic, please.

WHITE WINE 1 ounce of this nectar of the gods has 26 cal, 0 grams of fat, and only 3 grams of carbs!

Compare this with 1 ounce of plain, low-fat yogurt: 18 cal, 0 grams of fat, and 2 grams of carbs. Sure you can save a few calories opting for the yogurt, but where's the fun in that?

RUM 1 ounce of this palate pleaser has 65 cal, 0 grams of fat, and 0 carbs!

Let's compare this with the vegetarian delight, 1 ounce of meatless sausage (a.k.a. tube-shaped soy beans): 73 cal, 15 grams of fat, and 3 carbs! Well, this one's not rocket science. MAKE MINE A DOUBLE!

I think you can see where I'm going with this. So keep it light, stay away from the creams and liqueurs, and have fun. Oh, and garnish everything with a nice big stick of celery—at only 4 calories per ounce, it's a great way to get your recommended greens for the day.

I hate my kankles
KAMIKAZE

2 ounces raspberry flavored vodka

3 ounces unsweetened mandarin juice (or pick your fave juice)

1 teaspoon honey (or 1 package sweetener)

1 cup ice

Shake all the ingredients and strain into a tall glass of ice. Garnish with a 15 km hike. Yeah, WHATEVER!

If you have the unfortunate medical condition "bloatedankleitis," there are a couple of key things you need to stay away from:

1 Those cute ankle wrap sandals you saw on sale last week. No need to put a bow around your kankles, even though they were a genetic gift from your Aunt Ruby.

2 Ankle bracelets. We don't want to accentuate this problem area with a little Bling Bling. Besides, they're called Anklets, not Kanklets.

control top
COSMOPOLITAN
… with a twist of *I can't feel my legs*

2 ounces raspberry vodka

4 ounces sugar-free grapefruit juice

1 cup ice

Shake all the ingredients and strain over a tall glass of ice. Garnish with a few fresh raspberries.

This cocktail must have a side of the most expensive, suck you in, lift you up, smooth you out, I-am-now-a-size-0 pantyhose. Just keep in mind that even though you have tamed the tummy, thinned the thighs, and placed your butt somewhere God never intended it to be, exposing some sort of a midriff is still a big no-no.

who shrunk my belt?
BELLINI

1 ½ ounces vodka (or flavored vodka)

2 ounces chilled water with 1 packet sweetener

2 ounces lime juice

6 large cubes of fresh watermelon

1 cup smashed ice

Add all the ingredients to a blender and blend until smooth. Pour into a tall chilled glass and garnish with a chunk of watermelon.

Oh, I hate it when this happens. How did my belt end up in the dryer? There is nothing else you can add to this drink, except a new belt.

butt cleavage
COSMOPOLITAN

2 ounces raspberry vodka

3 ounces light lemonade

1 cup smashed ice

Shake all the ingredients and strain into a martini glass. Garnish with fresh raspberries, a lemon wedge, or 2 excruciating minutes on the Stairmaster.

Riddle me this: why is the cleavage on my butt surpassing the cleavage on my chest? If I was to throw a push-up bra on my buttocks and wear it on my chest, I would be the envy of women everywhere. I denounce eating only three saltines a day in an effort to lose my buxom bottom. Instead I choose to slather my saltines with Cheese Whiz, enjoy a fantastic cocktail, and shake what my mama gave me: one hip booty. If it's good enough for J Lo, it's good enough for me.

I have searched high and low for some sort of contraption at the gym to work out my double chin, but no luck. Apparently Pilates of the face has yet to catch on. I look after myself and do all the right things; where does this extra piece of human tissue come from? I'm of the belief that the tissue under your chin is somehow connected to that on your breasts, and we know where they're going! South! Due South! Sunscreen anyone?

say allo to ma double chin
CRANTINI

2 ounces sparkling white wine

1 ounce low-cal cranberry juice

1 ounce low-cal white grape juice

1 cup smashed ice

Shake all the ingredients together and strain into a martini glass. If you're using regular white wine, add a splash of soda water for a little effervescence (that's my fancy word for bubbles).

I'll just have a salad
SLING
… with a pinch of hunger pains

    1 cup smashed ice

    2 ounces vodka

    2 ounces sugar-free white grape juice

    2 ounces sparkling water (sugar-free berry flavored is very tasty)

Add the ice to a large wine goblet, pour the vodka and grape juice overtop, and stir. Top with the sparkling water. Garnish with the crazy idea that the salad you're eating tastes like a cheese burger and fries.

This drink always compliments the latest diet craze you're on. So whether you're staying away from eating anything of a certain color, owning your zone, best friends with Jenny, or hitting the Beach somewhere South, enjoy this low-cal libation.

slim sloe
GIN FIZZ

1 ½ ounces lemon gin

1 packet sweetener

1 cup ice

3 ounces soda water (or any sparkling water)

Shake the gin, sweetener, and ice together and strain into a large glass of ice. Top with soda water and garnish with a lemon wedge.

Remember ladies, much like becoming a supermodel, this drink is a process—a "SLOE" process. With one part "I'm retaining water," two parts "my gym membership expired," and a twist of a "thyroid problem." We're all a work in progress.

does this make me look fat?

FRUIT PUNCH

… with a pinch from a body girdle

1 ounce vodka

1 teaspoon honey (or 1 packet sweetener)

3 ounces low-cal juice (pick your fave, mine is white grape)

   or juice from sugar-free crystal packets

juice from 1 freshly squeezed lime

1 cup ice

Shake all the ingredients together. If you're using honey, give it a really good shake (and you can say you worked out today). Strain into a tall glass of ice.

If I had a nickel for every time I wondered if something made me look fat, I would be rich enough to tell Donald Trump "YOU'RE FIRED!" As hard as I try to banish the dreaded question "does this make me look fat?" from my brain, I think the thought is permanently etched somewhere in my cerebral cortex. I suggest you enjoy a couple of these cocktails, guilt-free, and just come to the conclusion that every other woman skinnier than you has thick ankles, bad teeth, and hairy knuckles.

sex on the beach
in a Muu Muu

2 ounces citrus vodka

2 ounces sugar-free cranberry juice

2 ounces pineapple juice

1 cup ice

Shake all the ingredients together and strain into a large glass filled with ice. Garnish with a slight buzzzzzzzzzzzzzz.

This cocktail has a two drink MINIMUM! Mix up a couple of these while you're marinating in your sunscreen, trying to tie your sarong, and wondering why a black bikini is not slimming. Then hit the beach with attitude and confidence, and, of course, suck in everything that can possibly be sucked. (Breathing is not an option.)

cheat day
COLADA

1 ½ ounces coconut rum

½ ounce melon liqueur

1 ounce pineapple juice

1 ounce lime juice

1 ounce orange juice

½ cup pineapple chunks

1 cup smashed ice

Put all the ingredients into a blender and blend until smooth. Pour into a large, chilled glass. Garnish with a pinch of chocolate sprinkles, just a pinch.

This drink is best served between Tuesday and Sunday. As l well know, we start our diets on Mondays. DO NOT serve this libation with a slice of guilt. Remember, Monday is just around the corner.

love your wobbly bits
JELLO SHOOTERS

1 packet grape Jello
½ cup vodka
½ cup cold water

Follow the instructions on the Jello package. Just remember to add only ½ cup of water, as you are replacing the other ½ with the nectar of the gods—vodka! When the Jello is firm, serve in fun shooter glasses.

These fun and tasty treats are always a hit for a night out with the girls. Remember to always serve them with the latest issue of a fashion mag, and garnish with snide comments on how the models have fat ankles and knobby knees.

I need to get in shape
SHANDY
… with a splash of procrastination

    3 ounces light beer
    2 ounces diet ginger ale
    1 cup smashed ice

Add all the ingredients to a large chilled glass. Garnish with a renewed gym membership.

Tomorrow, next week, next month, next year…I hate exercise, I have no time, I can't cook, I can't live without chocolate. So many excuses, so little time. I say, what's wrong with round? Round is a shape. Who wants be a size 2 when they can be a perfect 10?

I hope I've given you some fun, fresh, low-cal cocktail ideas. Just keep in mind that the old saying, "it's what's inside that counts," may be corny, but it's true. With a couple of these liquid libations "inside" you, you will feel nothing short of stunning. Like a fine wine, fine woman like us only get better with age.

Before I go any further in this chapter, this must be said: a true lady never goes trolling. The definition of trolling: to wander around searching for somebody. My personal definition? To sport an outfit long past its expiration date, wear too much eye makeup, and head to a bar frequented by adolescents you

Trolling cocktails

used to baby-sit—all in the hopes of gaining the affections of a boy-man for the evening, with the possibility of having a meaningful overnight relationship.

KEY POINTS Be prepared NOT to meet Mr. Right at your local watering hole. He's at the bar up the street (the one with the long lineup), it's raining, and your hair turned out just right. Don't risk it, go with the shortest lineup.

Never let a man who reminds you of your elementary school teacher buy you a drink. Or, for that matter, even get close enough to ask you if he can buy you a drink. That's naaaasssssty.

Always be on the lookout for the guy who can't grasp the English translation of "No." You know him ladies, he's the one who get's his pick-up lines from bathroom stalls.

"When I'm good, I'm very good.
But when I'm bad I'm better."

don't let me go home with him

DAIQUIRI

1 ½ ounces white rum

½ ounce melon liqueur

2 ounces lime juice

4 large fresh smashed strawberries (or frozen mix)

1 tablespoon brown sugar

1 cup smashed ice

Put all the ingredients into a blender and blend until smooth. Pour into a large glass rimmed with brown sugar. Garnish with a splash of protection.

The recipe for this drink CANNOT be altered in any way. Follow these instructions carefully: this libation must ALWAYS be accompanied by your girlfriend with the clearest judgment. Most importantly, listen to her!

GIMLET

… with a wedge of focus

1 ounce dark rum (white will always do, too)

1 ounce Cointreau

½ ounce cherry brandy

2 ounces lime juice

1 cup ice

Shake all the ingredients together. Strain into a sugar-rimmed rocks glass filled with smashed ice. (Smashing the ice is a good way to let off some steam.)

It's amazing how much better things (mainly men) look with beer goggles on. But since some of us don't enjoy barley in our diets, give this little cocktail a try instead. Just remember, moderation is key. Because without your trusty goggles, any Prince Charming you meet while trolling, may simply be a troll.

he has a mullet
MAI TAI
… with a slice of 80s flashback

1 ½ ounces rum

½ ounce melon liqueur

2 ounces lime juice

1 ounce orange juice

1 cup ice

Shake all the ingredients together and strain into a tall glass filled with ice.

Ladies, a mullet says a lot about a person. Mainly, that they are afraid of change. During the 80s, when mullets were a trend, these men were Gods, they were at their social peak. So now, in this wonderful new millennium, they'll do everything they can to hang onto their glory days. As long as you don't mind listening to the endless drones of old high school football tales and listening to classic rock, date on my friend, date on.

I always get the ugly friend
SHOOTER

    1 ounce vodka

    ½ ounce white tequila

    ½ ounce your fave liqueur

       (melon, sour apple schnapps, or blue curaçao)

    1 cup smashed ice

Shake all the ingredients together and strain into a shot glass. Garnish with some BEER GOGGLES.

Oh ladies, this drink is by no means my favorite. But, it is a rite of passage to becoming a good girlfriend. I recommend you find a cute bartender that will pour these liberally, and repeat often. Maybe his lisp and lazy eye will grow on ya. Remember, don't hate the player, hate the game.

ya...
I got carded
COSMOPOLITAN

1 ½ ounces gold tequila

2 ounces pineapple juice

1 teaspoon brown sugar

dash of vanilla extract

1 cup smashed ice

Shake all the ingredients together and strain into a large martini glass rimmed with brown sugar. Garnish with a wedge of *you go girl!*

You must chase this down with a shot for your ego. Walk tall, show off your ASSets, and go hit on the best looking guy in the bar.

why are all the men so short?
SLING

1 ounce gin

1 ounce strawberry liqueur

2 ounces orange juice

1 ounce lemon juice

1 cup smashed ice

Shake all the ingredients and strain into a TALL glass filled with ice. Garnish with a 6" stiletto.

Ladies, whether you are 5' 2" or can go one-on-one with an NBA star, you have no time for a guy with Short Man's Syndrome. So strap on your sexiest pair of heels, pat him politely on the head, give him those "there, there" eyes, and send him on his way.

I have shoes older than him
SOUR
... with a splash of cradle robbing

2 ounces flavored vodka (pick your fave)

2 ounces lime juice

juice from 2 freshly squeezed lemons

1 cup smashed ice

1 ounce soda water

Shake the vodka, lime juice, and lemon juice with the ice. Strain into a tall glass filled with ice and top with the soda water.

This cocktail is a tricky one. Should I? Shouldn't I? If you were a man dating a younger woman, this drink would be called "ABSOFREAKINLUTELY on the rocks." I firmly believe it's up to you; it all depends on what you're looking for. If it's a meaningful overnight relationship, then I say give 'er. If it's a long-term marriage, mortgage, family type of relationship you seek, I suggest dating someone who doesn't talk about his prom in the present tense.

This can be a touchy subject (pun intended). Don't be embarrassed, we women have needs and cannot survive on a shoe fetish alone. So if you're too embarrassed to indulge in a modern day ADULT appliance, use what ya have! Overload the washing machine, hit the spin cycle, and hop on. I guarantee you'll never have more fun doing the laundry. A word of caution if I may: DO NOT make this choice at your local laundromat (and I speak from experience). Now that was embarrassing.

dry spell
MARTINI
… with a wedge of 9 volt battery

1 ounce vodka

½ ounce raspberry liqueur

½ ounce blue curaçao

1 ounce lemon juice

1 cup smashed ice

Shake all the ingredients and strain into a martini glass, on or off the rocks. Garnish with a twist of satisfaction.

he has man boobs
MARGARITA

1 ounce lime flavored vodka (unflavored works just as well)

1 ounce blue curaçao

1 ounce lime juice

2 ounces grapefruit juice

1 cup smashed ice

Place all the ingredients in a blender and blend until smooth. Serve in a chilled glass with a salted or sugared rim.

This cocktail has great flavor and goes down nicely. However, just the fact that a cocktail of this name exists makes me a little queasy. Having man boobs is totally acceptable, when you're eighty! (When you've been around him longer than dirt, you can grow to love his wobbly bits.) But for a young adult male, there is just no excuse. And to show them off with a skin-tight black baby-tee? For goodness sakes man, have you no self respect?

didn't you date my friend?

DAIQUIRI
... with a slice of déjà vu!

1 ounce vodka

1 ounce blue curaçao

3 ounces pink lemonade

1 cup smashed ice

Put all the ingredients in a blender and blend until smooth. Garnish with a slice of *learn from your friend's mistake.*

As painful as it is, you always have to play this one out. It seems necessary to play the game, to see if this guy has somehow morphed into a doctor or a lawyer, even though you know full well he was an unemployed "artist" just six weeks ago when he was dating your friend. This scenario is good for at least two free drinks, then break the bad news that you know he still lives with his parents.

are all his tattoos spelled correctly?

CRANTINI

1 ounce tequila

1 ounce Triple Sec

2 ounces cranberry juice

1 ounce lime juice

1 cup smashed ice

Shake all the ingredients together and strain into a martini glass, on or off the rocks. Garnish with a wedge of lemon. If you have no Triple Sec, no problem; make it 2 ounces of tequila and add a splash of o.j.

I'm not saying there's anything wrong with tattoos; I have a couple of strategically-placed ones myself. I'm merely saying that if a man has more skulls and four-letter words inked on his body than you see in the subway, you may want to rethink the whole future father of my children scenario.

the two-coat mascara
MANHATTAN

1 ½ ounces rye

½ ounce dry vermouth

1 cup ice

Shake all the ingredients together and strain into a rocks glass over ice.
You'll need a cherry for this one.

I recommend you serve this libation with an I'm-the-bitch-that-owns-the-block
attitude. Face it, you work hard, you partake in random acts of kindness,
and you always give your seat up on the subway. Tonight is your night! You're
going to drink, dance, flirt, and make every other woman in the bar think
you're a bitch (but wish they could be you). Why not? You've earned it.

how did I get home?
STINGER
… with a dash of short-term memory loss

1 ½ ounces vodka

½ ounce peppermint schnapps

2 ounces lemon juice

1 cup smashed ice

Shake all the ingredients together and strain into a sugar-rimmed martini glass. Garnish with a quick glance around the room to ensure you know where you are!

I have to say that with this cocktail, it's critical to have a great wingman (or even wingmen). Girls, I know first-hand, we all need to let loose and throw it down old school style. Just make sure to work it out with your wingman ahead of time, so that you get home safe. This way, when you wake up the next morning, swearing that you will never, ever, drink again, you:

1 won't wake up naked in a bus shelter;

2 won't have any body parts pierced or tattooed;

AND ABOVE ALL, YOU

3 won't have a sex tape circulating over the World Wide Web.

take a
LONG ISLAND
… walk off a short dock

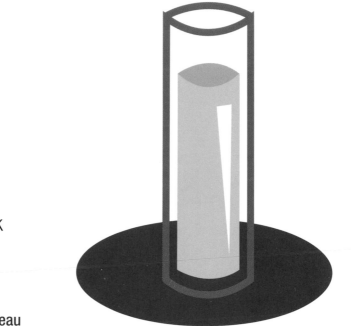

1 ounce vodka

½ ounce gin

½ ounce Cointreau

1 teaspoon sugar

1 ounce lemon juice

1 cup ice

3 ounces cola

Shake all the ingredients together, except for the cola. Strain into a tall glass over ice, and then top with cola. Garnish with a backbone.

Don't be afraid to tell the guy with the mullet and the lazy eye that you're NOT interested. Besides, you're not going to waste a perfectly good makeup application for this.

catfight
KAMAKAZEE

1 ounce gin

1 ounce Galliano

3 ounces lemon juice

1 cup ice

Shake all the ingredients together and strain into a tall glass with ice. Garnish with a tetanus shot.

Just so it's clear, I DO NOT promote violence in any way. But let's face the facts, we know there's always that girl at the bar. Make sure this drink is shaken, not stirred, and always cheers to your victory when you've talked her into believing you're a black belt in Tae Bo! You go, Young Grasshopper.

sillies on parade
PUNCH
… with a wedge of cleavage you could park a bike in

1 large watermelon

4 ounces vodka

2 ounces sour apple schnapps

2 ounces pomegranate liqueur

4 ounces blue raspberry mix

(non-alcoholic, available at your local grocery store)

2 whole grapefruits

2 whole limes

Cut the watermelon into cubes and place in a large pitcher or punch bowl. Add all the liquid ingredients. Juice the grapefruits and limes, then add their juice to the punch bowl. Stir it all up and let it marinate overnight in the fridge. Serve in a martini glass and garnish with a chunk of the now highly potent watermelon. You can always use the watermelon shell in lieu of a punch bowl for an added WOW factor. This punch serves 6.

This is most definitely in my top five favorites. I serve this drink when I'm going out for a night on the town with the girls. So push 'em up, strap 'em up, tape 'em up, whatever it takes to get your sillies front and centre. After all, as another one of life's cruel jokes, the shelf life on our sillies is similar to that of a Hollywood marriage. So quick, jump up and down on your couch and have your own "Ahaaaaaa" moment. (This also helps make sure your sillies are secure.)

ex marks the spot
SCREWDRIVER
... with a slice of *thank heavens I'm having a good hair day!*

1½ ounces vodka

½ ouce gold tequila (extra kick)

3 ounces orange juice

1 cup smashed ice

Shake all the ingredients together and strain into a rocks glass filled with ice.

Whip up this cocktail for the dreaded "running into your ex for the first time" event. You know it's going to happen, so like a good boy scout, always be prepared. I say, walk right up to him, smile, and ask him how he's doing. Tell him how well you're doing. Oh, and don't forget to mention that you finally tried that "position" (wink, wink) that he was always asking you to try. Make sure you thank him, after you tell him how much you enjoyed it. SNAP. That's gonna leave a mark!

This chapter was all about having fun, I firmly believe you should never take life too seriously. Dating is meant to be fun and exciting, kinda like shopping for now spring pumps. Find your style, color, price range, and size, then try them on and walk around a little. Decide if you're sacrificing style for comfort (take it from me, never sacrifice the style). Style is the ZSA ZSA ZSOO, it's those butterflies in your stomach. Without those butterflies, you're just settling for an ugly pair of comfortable shoes. Besides, you can always pick those up the day after your wedding.

Glossary

BACK FAT: The flesh on your back just below your waist that is mysteriously expanding. Although this area is also known as love handles, I'm sure not feeling the love for these.

BLOATEDANKLEITIS: A condition causing the ankle to be the same size as the calf of the leg. Often a genetic trait passed down from some obscure relative.

BOY-MAN: A fine, strapping young lad who would have been in elementary school when you were in high school. Often used for meaningful overnight relations.

CARDED: Oh, how this word brings a gleam to my eye. This is when a wonderful door man at the best bar in the whole world asks you for I.D. You reply: "Oh my, do I look that young?"

CLINGY-GUY: By some freak of nature this guy is covered in two-sided tape. Somehow he quickly adheres to every part of your life. My advice? Run, Forest, run.

COMMITAPHOBE: This is a guy who can't commit to a long-distance carrier, let alone a relationship.

CONTROL TOP: Control is the key word here. What these silky torture devices control, I'm not sure. We always feel tight and tingly inside of them, but ladies, that tingly is the lack of circulation to your limbs. I recommend wearing these not longer than a five-hour period.

DUTCH: A polite way of saying, "I really don't like you enough to buy you dinner, I just thought you'll be fun to have around for a night." Going dutch is perfectly acceptable when you're in a relationship. Hell, I think us girls need to pick up the tab every now and then. But not during the crucial fresh dating period. And for heaven's sake—never on a first date.

DUMPER: This is when you are doing the breaking up. Not always easy, but sometimes very necessary. Try to be as nice as possible to avoid any embarrassing macho retaliation comments.

DUMPEE: This is when he is unfortunately breaking up with you. Remember, no tears, no crazy scenes, just dignity and decorum. Walk out with your head held high trying to decide which one of his cute friends you'll date first.

KANKLES: When your ankles and your calves are the same size. I say wear black socks. After all, black is slimming.

HAZING: When you torture yourself by sampling one, or even two, of everything on the buffet. It's always important to wear loose and comfortable clothing.

LYCRA: The shroud of the devil. Need I say more?

MALE EMOTIONAL OUTBURST: When a man can think of no better way of handling a situation than swearing and saying cruel things to you. Sometimes he even sheds tears, but that's only in the rarest of breeds. If this happens, it's always best to just walk away.

MAN BOOBS: These are average B cup sized pockets of flesh on an otherwise fairly fit man chest. Somewhat of a naaaasssty anomaly if I do say so myself.

MUU MUU: A large, tent-like dress, fabricated to cover a multitude of sins. I suggest you stay away from bold, loud prints—monochromatic is always best.

MULLET: A somewhat popular hair cut in the 80s. Short and all business in the front, long and all party in the back. Also known in some circles as Hockey Hair.

MR. PERSONALITY: The great guy that everyone wants to set you up with, but no one will date themselves.

MR. RIGHT: No meaning appears for this word in any dictionary. As far as I'm concerned, he's an urban myth.

NAAAASSSSSSTY: Term to describe something bad. Not, "my coffee is too strong" bad, more like "10 day old potato salad left out in the sun" bad.

OUT-CALL: When your wingman gives you the fake "emergency at home" phone call during your dreaded first date (and you're really just making plans on where to hook up after you escape this date from hell).

POE: This is worse than poor. This is when a guy is a type of nomad moving from one friend's couch to another. He never invites you to his place, always "forgets his wallet," and wants to know if you can loan him twenty bucks.

PRE-DATE: The time you spend primping and getting your game face on before your date. This time is best spent with girlfriends, alcohol, and dating horror stories.

PRINCE CHARMING: A fictional man who wears tights and a puffy shirt. Remind me again why we're all looking for him?

SHORT MAN SYNDROME: Similar to the "God" complex. This guy, however, comes up only to your bustline and still acts like he's "king of the world!" I suggest you wear your highest heels, just to remind him how short he really is.

SILLIES: Simply put: your breasts. This term is usually reserved for those made of silicone, but I happen to like the word. Breasts are a little silly, so have fun with them; men always do, now it's our turn.

SKINNY JEANS: These are the jeans you wore before the big break-up of 2001, or the breakdown of 2001. The pre pint-of-ice-cream-a-day-and-midnight-fridge-raids pair of jeans.

SMASHED ICE: This is simply crushed ice, but crushing it is the fun part. Place a cup of ice in a plastic baggy, wrap it in a small towel and beat the hell out of it. There, now don't you feel better?

SUPERMODEL: Stick bitch! Too harsh? Okay, beautiful, skinny girl with thick ankles and a naaaasssssty rash somewhere I can't speak of.

THAT GIRL: We all know her; she's the one who told your grade five crush that you still wet the bed. Never show fear around her, stare her straight in the eyes, and show her what a real woman looks like.

WINGMAN: This is your gal pal who always has your back. She is always good to run interference, and place out-calls when needed.

WOBBLY BITS: The body parts that jiggle a little when we walk. My advice is to love them, embrace them, and hide them at all costs!

ZSA ZSA ZSOO: This is my favorite word of all time. It's the funny feeling you get when you're around him. It's the butterflies in your stomach, the sweaty palms, the cheesy love song playing in your head. It feels like coming over that first big hill on a rollercoaster. Oh ladies, this is what all the fuss is about!

Go out and enjoy life. Most importantly, be yourself.

Index

Index